Law Enforcement and Oathkeepers:

A Cop's Thoughts

by

Jerry Boyd, MS

Chief of Police, Retired

Cover photo used with permission of:
Paul Jacobsen
www.tactical-graphic-design.com

Disclaimer

The opinions herein, based upon the author's professional education, training, and experience, do not reflect the official position or opinion of the Oath Keepers organization nor that of any law enforcement agency for which the author has worked or does work.

About The Author

Jerry Boyd has fifty years of public safety service, primarily in law enforcement. He has served in ranks including Reserve Deputy Sheriff, Reserve Commander, Deputy Sheriff, Sergeant, Lieutenant, Captain and Chief of Police. He has served with the following law enforcement agencies: Los Angeles County Sheriff's Department; Irvine, California Police Department; Coronado, California Police Department; Martinez, California Police Department; Baker County Oregon Sheriff's Office; Baker City, Oregon Police Department.

Fifteen of Jerry's years of full time law enforcement service were spent as a Chief of Police. He currently serves as Reserve Commander for a local law enforcement agency. In addition to law enforcement, he has served as an Emergency Services Mutual Aid Communications Coordinator with the State of California Office of Emergency Services; Chief of a Rural Fire/Rescue agency in Shasta County, California; and as Director of the Baker County, Oregon, Consolidated 9-1-1 Dispatch Center.

Jerry has served as an instructor at numerous law enforcement training academies, the State of California Commission on Peace Officer Standards and Training Supervisory and Management courses, colleges and universities and the Western State University College of Law.

Jerry Boyd has authored over 4 dozen articles published in public safety journals, and has authored nine previous books – the majority of them focused on law enforcement issues. He holds a Master of Science Degree in Criminal Justice Administration from California State University, Long Beach.

Jerry's recent and currently available books (print and Kindle) are available on Amazon:

Firestone Park: Policing South-Central Los Angeles

From The Chief: Frank Commentary on Current Law Enforcement Issues

The Second Seven: The Journey Continues (A sequel to Firestone Park)

Table of Contents

INTRODUCTION

The Law Enforcement Code of Ethics has existed for decades, and most law enforcement officers in the United States subscribe to that oath early in their careers. I did when I graduated from the Los Angeles County Sheriff's Academy in the 1960's. In addition to that Oath, when an officer is employed by an agency he or she takes an Oath similar to that taken by members of our military. It is an Oath to uphold, support and defend the Constitution of the United States and the Constitution of the particular state in which the Deputy or Officer practices his profession. I have taken that oath multiple times.

Shortly after my appointment as Chief of Police in Coronado, California, in 1981, I was encouraged by other Chiefs in San Diego County to join two organizations which, at the time, purported to represent professional chiefs of police. I joined them. One is the International Association of Chiefs of Police (IACP), and the other is the California Police Chiefs Association (CPCA).

Over time, I noted that neither organization was conducive to my adhering to the Oath of Office I had taken at the outset of my career, and for that reason I withdrew from membership in both organizations. They, like too many other institutions and organizations, succumbed to political correctness before there was even a definition for that term.

Upholding, supporting, and defending the Constitution of the United States means *all* of the Constitution – not selected parts of it. Both IACP and CPCA took positions in direct opposition to the Second Amendment of the U S Constitution, and have since expanded their liberal – and in my opinion, incorrect – view to other positions in opposition to our nation's founding documents.

In my opinion as a professional peace officer, to this day there are only two organizations related in any way to the profession that I belong to. One is the Constitutional Sheriffs and Peace Officers Association, and the other is Oath Keepers. Both stress adherence to the Constitution, and that is important to both law enforcement officers and the citizens we serve. The Constitution is the foundation upon which a stable, free society must rest. Without it, we are doomed to a form of government in which the rights of citizens are ignored or suppressed, and where police officers, who are public servants, become instead oppressors of the very citizens they are entrusted to protect.

In this short booklet, I hope to accomplish several things. They are:

- To discuss, for the benefit of those who are *not* law enforcement officers, the proper role of the police, and how, as responsible citizens, through membership in groups such as Oath Keepers, they can complement the work done by our nation's one million law enforcement personnel.
- To discuss, for the benefit of law enforcement, the objectives of Oath Keepers, and to underscore the need for mutually supportive relationships between police and citizens.
- To discuss why police use certain equipment, tactics, and techniques; and to dispel citizens' concerns that even when employed by **Constitutional Peace Officers** those things are somehow threatening.
- To suggest appropriate activities that members of Oath Keepers should consider engaging in, both to insure that law enforcement remains committed to its Constitutional objectives and to be supportive of the profession which protects them from those who would trample on their rights.
- To discuss some (but not nearly all) aspects of how Oath Keepers can organize to be self-sufficient when the SHTF ("stuff" hits the fan).
- To discuss, from a realistic point of view, a communications system which works to keep members in touch with each other when the SHTF.

I hope that I accomplish my purpose. More important, I hope any law enforcement officers reading this book might be reminded of their proper role in a Constitutional Republic, and fight against those in the current Washington DC regime who would use cops for an illegitimate, totalitarian purpose. I also hope that citizens who might have an inappropriate fear of all law enforcement officers come to realize that the vast majority of cops, especially at the street level, are committed to the preservation of rights to which individual citizens are entitled under a system of government which has worked well for over 200 years.

CHAPTER ONE:

Law Enforcement's Role in a Free Society

Law enforcement in this country has, over many decades, adopted various phrases to describe its mission. Perhaps the first was the Los Angeles Police Department's "Protect and Serve". Many adaptations of that have arisen since LAPD adopted it. The message, however, is the same. The mission of law enforcement is to protect citizens from those in our society – criminals – who who would victimize them. In so doing, cops are simultaneously protecting the *rights* to which citizens are entitled under our system of government.

In enforcing the law, the police must adhere to the "rules" as enumerated in our Constitution and the Bill of Rights. The court system "polices the police" and ensures that police operate in a constitutionally correct manner. The Supreme Court's ruling in the *Miranda* case, for example, was based upon the court's view that law enforcement was not adequately protecting the right of citizens, even those suspected of serious criminal offenses, not to be forced into self-incrimination. There are other cases which have been decided at the Supreme Court level that similarly give direction to law enforcement – all with the intent of protecting the rights of citizens.

During my fifty years in law enforcement, I have been privileged to work with dozens of law enforcement agencies across the country. I have met thousands upon thousands of America's "thin blue line". It is my opinion that the vast, vast majority of those Deputy Sheriffs, Police Officers, and State Troopers adhere to the "rules", particularly those related to the constitutionally protected rights of the citizens they serve. They will admonish even the most violent, evil murderer of his/her constitutional rights before questioning; they will obtain warrants before searching when necessary to protect citizens from "unlawful and unwarranted searches and seizures". Only a foolish cop, and there are a few, would ever intentionally engage in an act that s/he knows would jeopardize a solid case.

In addition to protection of the public, which often comes in the form of enforcing laws, there is also the service aspect of the profession. That takes many forms – from giving directions to a lost motorist, to summoning a tow truck for someone whose car has broken down, to directing traffic at a busy intersection, and on and on. Sometimes protection and service are both provided in the same incident. I'll discuss this in more detail in a chapter to follow, but let's use the armed, barricaded suspect inside a house in a residential subdivision as an example.

In such a potentially deadly situation, officers respond in order to enforce the law and take a criminal offender into custody. At the same time, they have a duty and obligation to protect innocent people in surrounding residences who may be in the suspect's "field of fire" and, thus in physical danger. Officers provide that protection by evacuating those people to a place of safety, like a nearby school for example. They then insure that those people are "served" when the need arises. Food, water, cots, counselors, etc., are brought into evacuation centers based upon the needs of citizens.

Good cops protect and provide service with as much zeal and attention to detail as they expend arresting wanted felons – though I will say in all candor the latter is sometimes more motivating than the former. But the point is this: good cops do what needs to be done on behalf of the public without consideration of race, color, creed, economic position, or any other factor. Historically, that is the way it has been and, hopefully, it will continue to be so.

As a point of interest to those readers who are not cops but are Oath Keepers, let me share an observation. Historically, most cops and most Oath Keepers have some things in common. Both tend to be conservative; both tend to fully support the second amendment of the United States Constitution; and both tend to understand that citizens have rights guaranteed to them under our system of government. Thus, until recently, most cops had no interest in such things as firearms confiscation, bans on "assault weapons" (whatever they are), or limitations on the capacity of firearm magazines. Most cops supported the rights of law abiding citizens to obtain a concealed firearm permit. I believe that most cops still do support those things. Unfortunately, in some cases, police *leaders* do not. That is a matter of concern to me, and should be to members of Oath Keepers. There is something you can – and *should* – do about that. The key is to "do something about that" in a way that is productive, not disruptive.

Too many modern so-called police leaders have abandoned their Oath of Office, ignored the Peace Officers Code of Ethics, and succumbed to that which is destroying America as many of us know it: political correctness. Such people have bought into the totally erroneous and misinformed propaganda that guns are bad. Some have even gone so far as to justify, in their own minds, that warrantless searches to confiscate firearms from law-abiding citizens are somehow "okay". It is *not* "okay". Maybe it's "okay" in third world, communist dictatorships, but not *here*, not under our system of government, and not under our Constitution.

The deadly illness of political correctness to this point is confined to jurisdictions, usually large urban ones, predominantly "ruled" by liberal politicians. We have big city police chiefs in cities like Washington DC, New York, and others, who parrot the liberal mantra that guns are bad and must be restricted, if not removed entirely. Fortunately, most smaller city Chiefs, particularly in rural America, and most Sheriffs, do not share the unconstitutional perspective of their big city counterparts. They are not beholden to a presidential administration, including a US Department of (in) Justice which, by its own statements, believes that our Constitution is an impediment to the implementation of their agenda.

What to do about it? Exercise your rights as a citizen and VOTE. Exercise your rights as a citizen and write to your elected representatives demanding that they adhere to the Constitution. Appear at city council or county commission meetings and voice your opinion – in respectful, well-reasoned, and non-emotional ways. Contribute to groups, individuals, and organizations (such as Oath Keepers) which promote respect for our Constitution, and adherence to it by elected officials.

CHAPTER TWO:

The Law Enforcement Code of Ethics

I reproduce here, in its entirety, the Law Enforcement Code of Ethics. I do this for two reasons. First, as a reminder to my fellow officers; and second, so that readers who are not cops know what their police have pledged to do on their behalf. This code has been in existence for decades – long before I became a cop. At the state, county and city level there are very few cops who have not taken this pledge. At the federal level? Frankly, I don't know. By their word and example too many law enforcement officers from federal law enforcement agencies give the impression that have never heard of it – and that is tragic.

LAW ENFORCEMENT CODE OF ETHICS

As a law enforcement officer my fundamental duty is to serve mankind; to safeguard lives and property; to protect the innocent against deception; the weak against oppression or intimidation; and the peaceful against violence or disorder; and to respect the Constitutional rights of all men to liberty, equality, and justice.

I WILL keep my private life unsullied as an example to all; maintain courageous calm in the face of danger, scorn, or ridicule; develop self-restraint; and be constantly mindful of the welfare of others. Honest in thought and deed in both my personal and official life, I will be exemplary in obeying the laws of the land and the regulations of my department. Whatever I see or hear of a confidential nature or that is confided to me in my official capacity will be kept ever secret unless revelation is necessary in the performance of my duty.

I WILL never act officiously or permit personal feelings, prejudices, animosities or friendships to influence my decisions. With no compromise for crime and with relentless prosecution of criminals, I will enforce the law courteously and appropriately without fear or favor, malice or ill will, never employing unnecessary force or violence and never accepting gratuities.

I RECOGNIZE the badge of my office as a symbol of public faith, and I accept it as a public trust to be held so long as I am true to the ethics of the police service. I will constantly strive to achieve these objectives and ideals, dedicating myself before God to my chosen profession…law enforcement.

As citizens we have every right to expect our police to adhere to the above quoted Code. For most of our history, they have done so in admirable fashion, often under dangerous and adverse circumstances. However, today, driven by political correctness, some "top cops" and some jurisdictions do a poor job of living up to the standards contained in the Code of Ethics. Let me provide a few examples.

Example #1: The police are expected to protect the peaceful against violence or disorder. In the recent, much discussed, killing of a Black thug (Michael Brown) by a Ferguson, Missouri, police officer, the duly constituted (and very Constitutionally correct) Grand Jury found no basis for indicting the police officer. People rioted and, by their actions of looting and burning, destroyed businesses owned by people whom law enforcement had a duty to protect against such violence. Yet, in large measure, law enforcement stood by and let the violence occur.

Example #2: Per the Code, law enforcement officers are committed to not compromising with crime. In the State of California, it is an offense to drive a motor vehicle without current insurance. That state's laws provide for vehicles thusly operated to be towed and impounded until insurance is obtained. Solely for reasons of political correctness, the Los Angeles Police Chief has directed his officers *not* to tow such vehicles *if operated by illegal aliens.*

Example #3: Speaking of illegal aliens, the law allows local law enforcement to detain such persons (they are criminals!) for purposes of handing them over to federal agents for deportation. Many local agencies decline to do so. Where is compliance with the "no compromise for crime" standard within such agencies?

In short, we now have some leaders of some police agencies that not only fail to comply with the Code of Ethics, and who ignore their Oath of Office, but have set themselves up as arbiters of what laws to pick and choose to enforce. If a law enforcement officer doesn't like a law, or doesn't think it is Constitutional or should be enforced, then that officer should seek to change the law through the legitimate channels available for that purpose. As long as something is a matter of law, however, law enforcement officers have a **duty** to enforce it. If they cannot do that, they should do the honorable thing and get out of law enforcement.

CHAPTER THREE:

Oath Keepers

Founded in 2009, Oath Keepers' initial membership (I was an early member) was composed primarily of current and former military and law enforcement personnel who put their Oath to uphold, support, and defend the Constitution of the United States as their highest priority. Since its founding, many like-minded citizens with no military or law enforcement background have joined. Oath Keepers has spread to every state, and many states have Oath Keeper Chapters in each county or parish. For more information about the organization go to www.oathkeepers.org

Because it is relevant to this discussion, Oath Keeper's "10 Orders We Will NOT Obey" follows:

1. **We will NOT obey orders to disarm the American people.**
2. **We will NOT obey orders to conduct warrantless searches of the American people.***
3. **We will NOT obey orders to detain American citizens as "unlawful enemy combatants" or subject them to military tribunal.**
4. **We will NOT obey orders to impose martial law or a "state of emergency" on a state.**
5. **We will NOT obey orders to invade and subjugate any state that asserts its sovereignty.**
6. **We will NOT obey orders to blockade American Cities, thus turning them into giant concentration camps.**
7. **We will NOT obey any order to force American citizens into any form of detention camps under any pretext.**
8. **We will NOT obey orders to assist or support the use of any foreign troops on U.S. soil against the American people to "keep the peace" or to "maintain control.**

9. **We will NOT obey any orders to confiscate the property of the American people, including food and other essential supplies.**
10. **We will NOT obey any orders which infringe on the right of the people to free speech, to peaceably assemble, and to petition their government for a redress of grievances.**

Just one comment regarding warrantless searches: There are a couple of necessary and Constitutional exceptions to the need for a warrant prior to conducting a search. One applies if a law enforcement officer is in fresh pursuit of a known offender; and the other (more common) applies if a warrantless entry into a protected place is necessary to save a human life.

CHAPTER FOUR:

Some Considerations About Police Equipment

I offer the information in this chapter because I am aware that some people, including some members of Oath Keepers, have a negative perception about some equipment currently used by some police agencies. There is a perception that some of that equipment signifies the "militarization" of law enforcement, and that such equipment will be used by "the government" to suppress the rights of citizens.

During my years as a monthly columnist for *American Cop Magazine,* I addressed the issue of public perception and police militarization many times in my **From The Chief** column. That magazine ceased publication in August of 2014. However, all of my columns from that magazine are included in my book *From the Chief* which is available in both print and Kindle formats at Amazon Books. I've addressed the issue with cops, urging them to never use any equipment issued or personally owned in violation of the Law Enforcement Code of Ethics or their Oath of Office.

My columns in *American Cop* received more reader feedback than all other columns combined during the years the magazine was published. No columns received more feedback than the ones dealing with "militarization of law enforcement" and public perceptions regarding the potential for police suppression of citizens' rights. The feedback from cop readers made it overwhelmingly clear that US cops have absolutely no intention of being used by an oppressive government against the citizens we are sworn to protect.

About two years ago, *American Cop's* publisher ran a reader survey asking readers (police officers of all ranks) whether they would, if ordered, confiscate firearms from law abiding citizens. Over 98% of respondents (and this survey had higher participation than any other survey ever conducted by the magazine) not only said **NO,** but **Hell NO!**

If cops are not armored up to oppress the public then you may wonder why, unlike in the past, we see our local police and sheriffs personnel donning military-like uniforms, carrying patrol rifles (erroneously called "assault weapons") and in some cases having at their disposal Armored Personnel Carriers (vehicles) that look more suited for a war zone in Afghanistan. Let me give you an honest answer.

The environment in which today's police forces operate, in both urban and rural America, is different than at any time in our history. It is different not because of law abiding citizens like those likely to read this booklet. It is different because the liberal political climate which exists in much of the nation has made our world a more dangerous place. I am writing this on December 21st, 2014 just a day after two New York City Police officers were assassinated while they sat in their patrol car in Brooklyn. Yesterday, a Florida officer was also brutally murdered. With ten days left in 2014, officers killed in the line of duty are up over 10% compared to 2013. And no area of the country is exempt from increases in violent crime and increases in attacks on officers.

Want to know where to place the blame? Blame liberal politicians who have caused tens of thousands of serious (felony) criminal offenders to no longer be housed in state prisons where they belong. Blame an administration in Washington DC that refuses to close our porous southern border. We know for a fact that not only are human traffickers and drug runners taking advantage of our open borders, but so too are terrorist organizations such as ISIS, Hamas, and Hezbollah.

It is sad but true that cops from coast to coast, and in America's heartland as well, are running up against increasing numbers of suspects armed with high-powered rifles and weapons such as the prolific and potent AK-47 military carbine produced in communist bloc countries.

I will argue to anyone, even a fellow Oath Keeper if need be, that our police officers need – for their safety and the safety of law-abiding citizens – the maximum amount of physical protection reasonably available to them. The exterior vests now worn by many cops provide some protection against higher powered weapons that soft body armor hidden under the uniform shirt does not provide. Does that look military? Yes, but it also saves lives.

A police sidearm is no match for an AK 47, but an AR-15 in the hands of a trained user is. Does an officer carrying a patrol carbine look intimidating and "military"? Yes, s/he does, but if you were under fire by a deranged gunman in a school or shopping mall, the officer with an effective long gun rather than a simple handgun would be a welcome sight.

Now the big one: Perhaps no other item of equipment in use by law enforcement today has aroused as much suspicion as Armored Personnel Carriers (APC's). They have actually been around for a few decades in the form of vehicles specifically manufactured for use by civilian law enforcement. Two of the most common are the Bear and Bearcat, both manufactured by the Lenco Corporation. They have been a staple of law enforcement specialized teams such as SWAT and bomb disposal teams for years. Those marked only with the agency identifier (such as Boston Police) have been more generally accepted than those which include some reference to "Homeland Security". Because "Homeland Security" denotes often-suspect federal involvement, the reaction has been understandable.

Many such vehicles have been paid for over the years by federal grants (FEMA urban initiative grant, for example). Until about 2010, the federal grants to pay for such equipment did not require that they be conspicuously marked with the words "Homeland Security" or the logo of that agency. Now, however, that is often a requirement, and so the newer DHS-marked units generate more heartburn than identical ones without such markings.

An even more recent phenomenon has been the release under the Federal Excess Property Program of former military APC's , in particular MRAPS (Mine Resistant Ambush Protection). Those vehicles were widely used by our military in Iraq and Afghanistan. With the winding down of US involvement in those conflicts, many such vehicles were released for use by state, county, and local law enforcement agencies.

Armored Personnel Carriers in and of themselves should not be a problem. If I asked most Oath Keepers whether firearms in and of themselves are "bad", I suspect I would get a resounding "NO!" as an answer. Many subscribe to my belief that it is not the *tool* that is bad, but the use of a tool by a *fool* is bad. Guns don't kill people. Guns operated by people kill people and sometimes (war or self-defense) that is a good thing, and other times not. The same can be said of Bears, Bearcats, and MRAPS. There is nothing intrinsically wrong with such vehicles, unless they are used for an illegitimate or unconstitutional purpose. I made that point quite clear in several of my **From the Chief** columns.

How are such vehicles used appropriately and necessarily? They are used to transport emergency responders into a hazardous scene such as an armed, barricaded suspect who has fired or has threatened to fire on responders or other innocent citizens. They would be used inappropriately to intimidate a law-abiding citizen from whom they wished to unlawfully seize firearms. I am aware of plenty of times when they have been used for an appropriate purpose. I am not aware of any use of such vehicles for the latter, unconstitutional purpose.

In determining your reaction to such vehicles in your community, it is important to view them in light of the reputation of the agency which owns it, in terms of providing Constitutional law enforcement. If the agency never violates the rights of citizens, you have little to fear. If that is not the case, then perhaps fear is warranted. Be aware also that the media, in featuring articles on police use of such equipment, has their own agenda – and it is usually to paint law enforcement in the most negative way possible.

Just days ago there was a great furor not many miles north of me in the State of Washington, when the media discussed a local Sheriff's Department's acquisition of an MRAP with a Deputy from that agency. The Deputy made a horribly inaccurate comment about how the vehicle was needed because "we have a lot of armed Constitutionalists in our county". That comment did not sit well with local and regional Oath Keepers, nor should it have. In reality, the truth is that the area in question has a lot of armed "skinheads". Skinheads are *not* Constitutionalists. The second point, and one which eventually mitigated the concerns of Oath Keepers and others, is that the Sheriff (who has a strong reputation as a professional, Constitution-supporting elected official) quickly corrected the erroneous statement of his subordinate. He made it quite clear that Constitution-supporting citizens, armed or not, were not the reason for an MRAP. The Sheriff's solid reputation put all but the liberal media at ease.

A final point worth considering for those still concerned about such items of equipment: Nationwide, APC's are used just as frequently to transport civilian evacuees safely out of harm's way as they are for transporting armed police personnel *into* a danger zone. Many citizen lives have been saved and injuries prevented by use of such vehicles. If I were still a police chief today, I would seek to have such a resource available to serve the citizens of my community.

CHAPTER FIVE:

What Can Oath Keepers Do To Be Of Help?

In this chapter, I will discuss some activities Oath Keepers in various places have been involved in, as well as some other activities that the organization might find worthy of consideration. Let me again emphasize that these comments reflect my own opinion, and do not necessarily reflect the position of the Oath Keeper's organization. My opinions are based on fifty years of working with county and city government and on having learned what works and what doesn't.

1. My "bottom line" recommendation to Oath Keepers is to **stay focused on the mission and don't stray from it into other areas not directly related to the 10 Orders.** I offer that initial advice based upon what I know the reaction will be otherwise.

2. Unless an issue is of such overwhelming importance as to justify acting "officially" under the Oath Keeper name, stay away from issues outside the area your Chapter represents. If the state legislature is attempting to curtail rights of citizens under the Second Amendment, by all means travel to the state capital. Such an attempt by the legislature would directly impact all residents of the state. If another county makes such an attempt to restrict the rights of its citizens you might be tempted to join with another Oath Keeper chapter out of "solidarity". Take it from me, your involvement would likely do more harm than good. Local elected officials resent outsiders "meddling" in their business.

3. Keep your arguments, verbal or written, and any "protest demonstrations" peaceful and respectful. They are far more

effective (if it is possible to be effective at all) than boisterous arguing.

4. Do not engage in any action which could be viewed as "vigilante". You may disagree with me on this, but I will use Oath Keepers showing up in Ferguson, Missouri, to help protect businesses from rioters as an example of **what not to do.** Oath Keepers, while composed in part of persons with military and law enforcement experience, have no law enforcement authority. Let's say you engage in "security" duty, as they did in Ferguson, and you are attacked. In self-defense, you use deadly force. Who is going to pay for your defense? It is a liability issue, which is the very same reason law enforcement in Ferguson eventually objected to Oath Keepers providing security. By condoning it, they could be construed as giving tacit approval, which means they inherit some liability for Oath Keepers actions. No law enforcement agency is going to let that happen.
Finally consider this. You may have no problem with the training and discipline of your Oath Keepers group, but what about the armed "nut case" that comes in under the cover of Oath Keepers and does something unjustified? Say the word liability again. I know some Oath Keepers thought their Ferguson gig was good public relations. But what is good public relations isn't always good policy.

5. Make sure you act based upon facts, not rumors, and certainly not intentionally manufactured information designed to make Oath Keepers look foolish or to prompt Oath Keepers to take unwarranted action. Many (most?) in the media do not like Oath Keepers or what the organization stands for. They will intentionally misrepresent an issue for the specific purpose of baiting Oath Keepers (and other conservative groups) into reacting. The will use reacting to

something that does not exist as the basis for criticism in the eyes of the public.

CHAPTER SIX:

A Productive Oath Keeper Activity

In the many conversations I have had with active members of Oath Keepers, I have asked them to describe just what sorts of activities they are or anticipate being involved in that are consistent with the "10 Orders". Most describe activities which are slightly outside the box of the "10 Orders", but not activities that are without merit. Some wish to "assist" their local law enforcement agencies, but when asked how, they fumble for an answer. As individuals, there are certainly ways they can assist. Becoming a Reserve Police Officer or Deputy Sheriff is one way, but that is not an Oath Keepers "group activity". Any other *ad hoc* form of assistance to local law enforcement will likely not be productive. Law enforcement is a para-military profession. They don't suffer "wannabe's" or "groupies" or "hangers on" very well. Want to assist them? Join them and get trained by them through their organizational structure, but not as an official function of your Oath Keeper Chapter.

Others with whom I have spoken talk about preparation for things like martial law, economic collapse, and natural or man-made disasters. While in some circles, being a "prepper" is considered a negative, in my mind it is anything but that. I don't happen to believe that martial law is a realistic possibility – yet. But if the current anti-American regime in power in DC has its way…maybe. At present I think we can count on the rank and file in both the military and law enforcement to refuse to impose martial law on the American people. I hope and pray I'm right.

Economic collapse? Again if the current regime continues on its present path, I think economic collapse (intentionally caused by the regime) is a possibility. And, of course, a natural or human-caused disaster is always a possibility.

It is a time-honored principle in emergency management that one should take an "all risk" approach to individual, family, and neighborhood preparedness. That is, short of a nuclear event or catastrophic, non-survivable event (being in the primary fall out zone when the Yellowstone Caldera erupts, for example), a good preparedness plan and appropriate preparation will serve well regardless of the event. It is here that I think Oath Keepers has an important role related to, though slightly different from, its vow to not obey certain orders.

Emergency preparedness (which some call prepping) is something everyone in our society should take seriously, in my opinion. That can be done on an individual or individual family basis, whether through a formal organization (such as CERT—Community Emergency Response Team), or simply through informal networking with likeminded people. Oath Keepers, through its Chapter organizations, espouses a parallel program known as Community Preparedness Teams (CPT). Those are patterned after the military's Special Forces "A" Team. A program such as CPT can provide an excellent means of organizing people (members and their families/neighbors) on a small group, neighborhood basis. Oath Keepers can provide the organizational framework; it can coordinate activities; it can identify expertise among individuals; it can assign specific duties and responsibilities to individuals in various locations within the Chapter; and it can develop, test, and coordinate a communications system and plan for use when the SHTF.

An Oath Keepers Chapter wishing to be become involved in preparedness would do well to identify the expertise of each of its members, along with their family members who may not, themselves, belong to the Oath Keepers organization. Who has military or law enforcement expertise that can be useful in a security role when local law enforcement no longer exists or is too busy to look out for the safety of small neighborhood groups? Who has medical training (doctors, nurses, PA's, paramedics, EMT's, First

Responders)? (And, by the way, every Oath Keeper should have basic first aid/CPR training). Who will acquire and maintain medical supplies, including needed antibiotics to deal with infection?[1]

Who in the group has a good water source in the event the normal water supply is disrupted or contaminated? In rural areas, Chapter members may use wells for their water supply; but remember, if there is no electricity, getting water out of that well for human and animal use may be very difficult. A hand pump is one option. A generator which can power the well pump (via a change-over mechanism to switch from commercial power to generator power) is another approach. In areas where no members have wells, stockpiling water and water filtration devices may be the only option.

How about food? Again, in a non-rural area, stockpiling food may be the only viable approach. I won't go into that in detail as there are many prepper publications that thoroughly address this issue. In a rural, ranching/farming area there may be abundant sources of cattle and other livestock, chickens, and plenty of fruits and vegetables (depending on the time of year) to *supplement* food stores maintained by individual members. However, barter agreements to insure that producers will "share" are important, should be arranged prior to the calamity, and can often be brokered by a group like Oath Keepers. Hunting in some areas is also a viable food provision option, but the group needs to have pre-assigned members who know how to process and preserve harvested game.

Perhaps the key "member" of an Oath Keepers preparation/survival group is the communications coordinator/maintainer. When the SHTF, the cellular telephone service that most of us rely on day to day, as well as the hard-wired landline phone system probably will

[1] Note: many animal supply houses carry antibiotics that are **exactly the same** as those a physician might prescribe for a human patient. They are available without a prescription and generally are much less expensive than their identical product made for human use.

no longer be functional. Nor will the internet or any form of radio or television as we know it. Keeping each small neighborhood group within the larger Oath Keepers chapter in touch with one another may not just be critical to emotional survival, but crucial in terms of physical survival as well. The next chapter of this booklet will address communications in some detail.

CHAPTER SEVEN:

Communication – The Key to Survival

As anyone who has served in the military or public safety knows, the key to success in initiating and completing any mission, responding to any crisis, or surviving any catastrophe is reliable communications. In any situation or condition in which Oath Keepers will need to mobilize for safety and survival, the need for a dependable communications system will be of paramount importance. The exchange of information, perhaps critical to safety/survivable, over any distance requires the ability to communicate. To coordinate needed assistance (security, medical, etc.), or to re- stock needed supplies and foodstuffs requires the ability to communicate those needs to others within the Oath Keeper's chapter or organization. Remember, the "normal" communications channels we rely on today likely won't exist or, at the very least, will be sporadic and unreliable. Are there options? Yes.

I know that there is a movement within Oath Keepers to encourage members to become licensed by the FCC as Amateur Radio ("ham") operators. I have been a licensed ham for 57 years and hold an Extra Class license. I have taught ham radio licensing classes, and I am certified as a Volunteer Examiner to administer amateur radio licensing exams. In addition to my ham radio experience, I have been involved in public safety communications for most of my professional career. I have provided "expert testimony" in courts of law on communications issues, so I do know what I am talking about.

I have always encouraged people interested in becoming ham radio operators to do so – "IF". What is the "IF"? The "IF" is this: become licensed *if* you will use the privileges you are entitled to under the terms of the license you test and qualify for. If you will not use those privileges, then don't waste your time and money getting a license or a ham radio. Unless you use the radio (and you can only legally talk to other licensed hams on it), you will be unfamiliar with it when the SHTF, and it will be of no value to you. Unless everyone in a critical position within your neighborhood organization gets a ham license, unless everyone's radios are compatible, and unless everyone uses them enough to know their capabilities and limitations and maintain familiarity with them, they will be useless in an emergency. If the guidelines I just outlined can and will be met, then, yes, ham radios are a good tool to have available in times of emergency. If the s**t really does hit the fan on a national level, the whole issue of having an FCC license will, however, be a moot point. There will be no functional Federal Communications Commission to enforce the rules regarding amateur radio. In addition, existing law makes it clear that in a true emergency, a person may use any radio communications equipment available for purposes of summoning aid – no license required.

So, you say, not everyone in my group is willing to get a ham license; in fact, not enough are interested to make it worthwhile. What other options exist? Actually, several options exist, none of which require the effort to get a ham license. One option is Family Radio Service (FRS) handheld radios which are license free and available at many "big box" stores, Cabelas, etc., and on-line from multiple sources. You can often find FRS radios for less than $30 each, and they sometimes come in two packs in the $55.00 price range. FRS radios operate on the Ultra High Frequency band (450 MHZ +) and have multiple channels to select from. They are limited to very low (500 milliwatt) power output. Because of the very low transmit power on UHF frequencies, they are of very limited range, especially over uneven terrain. For that reason, I do not recommend them.

GMRS (General Mobile Radio System) hand held radios are very similar in power output and range to FRS radios though they cost just a bit more. They require a license. I don't recommend them for the same reason I do not recommend FRS radios.

The type of radio I do recommend for those who opt out of ham radio are MURS radios. MURS stands for Multi Use Radio System. These radios have five channels in the VHF (Very High Frequency) range, do not require a license, and have four times the output power as FRS radios. They can be found on E-Bay and elsewhere for as low as $50 each. They will provide better (but not perfect) coverage over a longer distance and more rugged terrain that the types of radios previously mentioned.

If I were to design a "communications system" for an Oath Keepers self-help team, I would use MURS radios and assign the five channels as follows:

> *Channel 1:* Command and Control: For use in coordination among various groups of Oath Keepers located within a region or chapter. It could also be used as an "itinerant" channel for Oath Keepers traveling out of their home area to make contact with local Oath Keeper groups. [2]
>
> *Channel 2:* Food/Water Coordination
>
> *Channel 3:* Medical Coordination
>
> *Channel 4:* Security Channel
>
> *Channel 5:* Open Talk Channel, for Oath Keeper neighbors to use to check up on each others' well-being.

Certainly there are other plans that could be designed. Again, that would be an undertaking more appropriate for Oath Keepers on the national level. However, if there were a nationwide master

---

[2] For this to be effective, it would require a nationwide Oath Keepers communications plan, which I recommend, but is beyond my ability to implement. Something for Oath Keeper "officials" to consider, however.

communications plan for the organization, members traveling especially during times of adversity would have some means to communicate and link up with Oath Keepers no matter where they might be.

I know of at least one state Oath Keepers organization that is urging members to purchase a specific radio. It happens to be a very inexpensive ($35 or so on the Internet) Chinese-made handheld. The specific model is the Baofeng UV5R. Other similar radios are manufactured in China as well, Wouxun being one of those other producers. These radios have both UHF and VHF capability.

The particular Oath Keepers organization that I am aware of encouraging the purchase of these radios has the best of intentions, but I think they are ill advised. First of all, these radios are very complex to program frequencies into. In order to do so without becoming frustrated, one needs programming software and cables, and that adds another $25 or so to the cost. Even with the software and cables, programming these radios is no easy task.

These radios do have a lot of capability. They operate on both VHF and UHF and can (properly programmed) operate on FRS, GMRS, MURS and some amateur radio frequencies. They can also operate on some frequencies used by law enforcement, fire and emergency medical agencies.

The "push" for this specific radio (based upon statements from an Oath Keepers Chapter with which I am familiar) is based upon the notion that when the SHTF, Oath Keepers with such radios can contact and coordinate with public safety agencies. Whoa! First of all, these are analog radios, and increasingly public safety agencies are moving to digital rather than analog. So being able to talk to cops and firefighters may not be possible with such radios. More important, however, is the fact that very few if any public safety agencies – even under SHTF conditions – will be very receptive to anyone who is not a cop or firefighter using their radios. In some places to do so is a criminal offense and my gut tells me that if Oath Keepers or any other "civilian" attempts to transmit on a public safety radio channel, no matter how busy the cops are, they will make time to arrest such a person.

EPILOGUE

Oath Keepers is a vital organization particularly given the direction of our government today. In my opinion, the organization can and will be effective in focusing attention on the Constitution but only if its members remain disciplined and centered on the 10 principles at the organization's core. It is critical, I think, for those in leadership positions within the organization to be ever vigilant to insure the organization is not used by those with a radical agenda which Oath Keepers does not support. I wish the organization well.

The author may be contacted via exlasd@msn.com

www.ingramcontent.com/pod-product-compliance
Lightning Source LLC
Chambersburg PA
CBHW072020290526
45787CB00013B/1524